358.4
EME

Emert, Phyllis

Transports and
bombers

$12.98

	DATE		
NO 0			
MAR 2			
NOV			
MY			

358.4
X EME

TRANSPORTS AND BOMBERS

PHYLLIS EMERT

WILD WINGS

JULIAN Ⓜ MESSNER

For Melissa Robyn Emert

The author wishes to acknowledge the Carruthers Aviation Collection, Sprague Library, Harvey Mudd College, Claremont, California, and express thanks to Nancy R. Waldman, Librarian, Sprague Library, for her help and cooperation in preparation of the *Wild Wings* series.

Library of Congress Cataloging-in-Publication Data

Emert, Phyllis Raybin.
    Transports and bombers / Phyllis Emert.
        p.   cm. – (Wild wings)
    Includes bibliographical references.
    Summary: Describes the specifications and uses of various transport and bomber planes, including the North American B-25 Mitchell, Boeing B-47 Stratojet, and Lockheed C-130 Hercules.
    1. Bombers—Juvenile literature.   2. Transport planes—Juvenile literature.   [1. Transport planes.   2. Bombers.
3. Airplanes.]
I. Title.   II. Series: Emert, Phyllis Raybin.   Wild wings.
UG1242.B6E44   1990
358.4′2—dc20
    ISBN 0-671-68961-4 (lib. bdg.)   ISBN 0-671-68966-5 (pbk.)
                                     90-31490
                                        CIP
                                        AC

Photo credits and acknowledgments

Pages 6 and 9 courtesy of McDonnell Douglas
Page 17 courtesy of Air Force Museum
Pages 4, 18, 21, 50, and 53 courtesy of North American/Rockwell
Pages 26, 29, 42, 45, 46, 49, 54, and 57 courtesy of Lockheed
Pages 10, 22, 30, 33, 34, 37, 38, and 41 courtesy of Boeing
Pages 58 and 61 courtesy of Northrop

CONTENTS

INTRODUCTION

Transports and bombers are similar in one major way. They both are built to carry things from one place to another.

Some transports airlift food and first aid to victims of natural disasters. Commercial transports carry freight and paying customers to the destination of their choice.

Military transports carry troops, equipment, weapons, and supplies to areas where a show of force is needed. Bombers carry bombs and missiles and drop or launch them at enemy targets.

During World War II, dropping bombs on specific targets by aiming through bombsights was called "precision bombing." The bomber usually flew at medium to high altitudes while dropping its payload over the target.

Continuous attacks on enemy population centers and industry which destroy their ability to continue fighting are called "strategic bombing." This was done successfully in World War II against Germany and Japan.

Today, with advanced enemy radar and surface-to-air missiles, high-altitude bombers could easily be shot down by the enemy. Instead, the modern bomber flies at low altitudes beneath enemy radar and launches short-range attack missiles. Or it launches air-launched cruise missiles, which guide themselves to the target from as many as 1,500 miles away. In that way the bomber doesn't need to fly over enemy territory.

The policy of massive nuclear retaliation keeps the superpowers in check today. It is understood that a nation committing an obvious act of war against another will be met by an outpouring of military force.

In non-nuclear wars, such as Vietnam during the 1960s and early 1970s, bombers still hit strategic targets, using radar to identify them.

Bombers have also been used in naval attacks and as photo-reconnaissance planes, gathering information and pictures of a particular area.

DOUGLAS DC-3 AND C-47

American—World War II, Late 1930s–1960s

SPECIFICATIONS

ENGINE:
Number: 2
Manufacturer: Pratt and Whitney
Model: DC-3—Twin Wasp R-1830-S1C3G 14 cylinder
　　　 C-47—Twin Wasp R-1830-92 14 cylinder
　　　 Rating: 1,200 horsepower each

ACCOMMODATIONS:
DC-3: • 21 passengers, mail and baggage
　　　　　 compartments
C-47: • 28 troops and 6,000 pounds of cargo
　　　　　　　　 or
　　　 • 18 stretchers and 6,000 pounds of cargo

DIMENSIONS:
Wingspan: 95 feet
Length: 64 feet, 5½ inches
Height: 16 feet, 11⅛ inches

OTHER INFORMATION:
Manufacturer: Douglas
Crew: DC-3—3　　C-47—5
Maximum Takeoff Weight: DC-3—25,200 pounds
　 C-47—29,300–31,000 pounds
Ceiling: About 23,500 feet
Maximum Range: DC-3—2,125 miles　　C-47—1,500 miles
Maximum Speed: 230 miles per hour

The Douglas DC-3 (its military version was the C-47) has been called "the greatest single airplane ever built." It changed the air transportation industry forever when it became the first plane to make a profit by carrying passengers.

The "Three" first flew in June 1936. It was big enough to carry 21 passengers, more than any other airliner at that time. Its two Pratt and Whitney Twin Wasp engines powered the DC-3 to cruising speeds of 200 miles per hour. This was fast enough to cut coast-to-coast travel time to 15–17 hours. It could fly high enough to cross the Rocky Mountains and its safety record was excellent. By 1940, 90 percent of the world's air passengers were carried by DC-3s.

When the United States declared war on Japan in 1941, the military chose the DC-3 as its main air transport. Douglas Aviation named it the Skytrain but the Air Force called it the C-47. Pilots affectionately referred to it as the "Gooney Bird." Whatever its nickname, more than 10,000 of them were built during the war.

The main difference between the two versions of the plane was the C-47's large cargo door on the side of the fuselage. Also, its frame and floor structures were reinforced to handle heavy weight. The crew of five included the pilot, copilot, navigator, radio operator, and engineer.

This "workhorse with wings" carried jeeps, bulldozers, and other vehicles, as well as ammunition, gasoline, food, medical supplies, and equipment. It could transport up to 28 paratroopers and 18 wounded in stretchers. The C-47 evacuated thousands of wounded soldiers and carried supplies to troops who had none. The "Gooney Bird" put a new word into people's vocabulary: "airlift."

These flying boxcars had no armor, no guns, and little maneuverability. They were slow-moving compared to the speedy enemy fighters. All during World War II, pilots and crews continuously risked their lives as they flew in low to drop their precious cargo.

When peace was declared in 1945, many of the C-47s became DC-3s again, carrying passengers. But the military continued to use the Gooney Birds. They airlifted supplies to Berlin during the Soviet blockade of 1948. A C-47 landed at the South Pole in 1956 and the Air Force used them in the Vietnam War into the 1960s.

BOEING B-17G FLYING FORTRESS
American—World War II

SPECIFICATIONS

ENGINE:
Number: 4
Manufacturer: Wright
Model: Cyclone 1820-97 9 cylinder
Rating: 1,200 horsepower each

FIREPOWER:
13 .50-caliber M-2 Browning machine guns and
6,000 pounds of bombs

DIMENSIONS:
Wingspan: 103 feet, 9 inches
Length: 74 feet, 9 inches
Height: 19 feet, 1 inch

OTHER INFORMATION:
Manufacturer: Boeing (BOH-ing)
Crew: 6 –10
Maximum Takeoff Weight: 65,000 pounds
Ceiling: 35,000 feet
Maximum Range: 1,100 miles, fully loaded
Maximum Speed: 300 miles per hour

The Boeing B-17 Flying Fortress was the world's first four-engine heavy bomber. There were many versions of the Flying Fortress, and it was always being improved. The last and most heavily armed of the series was the B-17G. It was produced in greater numbers and more were lost in combat than any other single bomber.

In the early years of World War II, B-17s flew by the hundreds from bases in England into the heart of Germany (more than 500 miles away) to make bombing raids over specific targets. They flew in tight formations without escorts to protect them from enemy fighters. This was because no Allied fighter had the range to fly so far and return.

The B-17s often suffered heavy losses from the enemy's anti-aircraft ground fire (flak). Many were brought down by enemy fighter planes in spite of the heavy firepower they carried. The German Messerschmitts used their superior speed and maneuverability in hit-and-run attacks. It wasn't until later in the war that American fighters like the P-51 Mustang acted as escorts on long-range bombing missions.

The B-17G was armed with 13 .50-caliber machine guns. A chin turret under the nose of the plane contained two remote-controlled guns manned by the bombardier. The turret was the clear Plexiglas half-globe in which the guns were mounted. Other machine guns were placed on each side of the plastic nose.

The top turret had two guns which were usually manned by the flight engineer. One manually operated machine gun fired through the top of the fuselage above the radio operator's compartment.

The waist gunners operated their two mounted machine guns out of openings on each side of the fuselage

between the tail and the wings. In the winter, blasts of icy air came through the open windows, making it very uncomfortable for the crew despite their heavily padded clothes and thick boots.

A ball turret with two machine guns stuck out below the fuselage. Two more guns were mounted in the tail section. The tail gunner protected the bomber's back end from surprise attacks. He sat in a cramped, cold Plexiglas compartment on a small hard seat. The tail gunner wore padded knee supports because he often operated the guns in a kneeling position.

The B-17s were rugged airplanes and took a lot of punishment in combat. Many flew their crews home safely with parts of wings or tails missing, engines blown away and bullet holes piercing the fuselage.

The B-17s were workhorses of the war. In Europe alone, Flying Fortresses dropped 640,036 tons of bombs on enemy targets.

CONSOLIDATED VULTEE
B-24J LIBERATOR
American —World War II

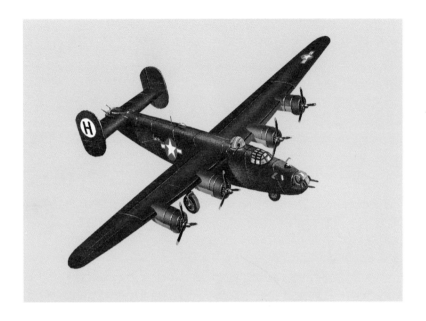

SPECIFICATIONS

ENGINE:
Number: 4
Manufacturer: Pratt and Whitney
Model: Twin Wasp R-1830-65 14 cylinder
Rating: 1,200 horsepower each

FIREPOWER:
10 .50-caliber machine guns and up to 8,000 pounds of bombs

DIMENSIONS:
Wingspan: 110 feet
Length: 67 feet, 2 inches
Height: 17 feet, 7½ inches

OTHER INFORMATION:
Manufacturer: Consolidated Vultee (later known as Convair)
Crew: 10
Maximum Takeoff Weight: Over 60,000 pounds
Ceiling: 28,000 feet
Maximum Range: 1,540 fully loaded
Maximum Speed: 297 miles per hour

More Consolidated Vultee B-24 Liberator bombers were built and used in World War II than any other American airplane. A total of 19,251 B-24s, which included over a dozen different models, were manufactured. The B-24J was the most widely used model.

The Liberator, along with the B-17 Flying Fortress, was used on most Allied bombing missions early in World War II. It had a greater range than the B-17 and carried a heavier bomb load. Powered by four Pratt and Whitney engines, the B-24 was armed with 10 .50-caliber machine guns.

The Liberator was easily distinguished from other aircraft by its twin tail rudders. Rudders are the flat, movable pieces of metal attached vertically to the back of the plane. They're used for steering left or right.

Early in the war American bombers flew unescorted daylight missions into enemy territory, and many planes were shot down. Fighter escorts made a big difference later in the war by providing protection from enemy fighters.

A typical mission in World War II was made up of 150 B-24s of the 8th Air Force. They flew in tight formation from their British base with a smaller number of B-17s. One of several targets was an airplane factory deep in German territory.

The bombers, escorted by P-51 Mustangs, were suddenly attacked by 50 enemy fighters! The Mustangs fought them off successfully and downed three.

The bombers safely reached their target areas. But no sooner did the bombardiers yell, "Bombs away," when dozens of Messerschmitts converged on the formation. Again the P-51s fought them off but this time two enemy fighters were able to get through.

"Bandits at 3 o'clock," shouted the tail gunner to his B-24 crew.

The gunners fired off round after round of ammunition as the enemy fighters dived, rolled, and climbed around the slower-moving four-engine planes.

The bombers flew tightly in their formations and the Messerschmitts were caught in a crossfire of bullets. Gunners from two different aircraft aimed their fire at one of the fighters. Suddenly it burst into flames.

"He's hit," shouted the tail gunner, "and he's going down! Score one for Uncle Sam."

"Bombardier, report," said the Captain.

"Bombs on target, Cap," he answered. "We've got a direct hit."

"Mission accomplished, boys. Let's head for home."

The B-24 Liberator scored more victories over enemy aircraft than any other Allied bomber in World War II.

NORTH AMERICAN
B-25 MITCHELL
American—World War II

SPECIFICATIONS

ENGINE:
Number: 2
Manufacturer: Wright
Model: Cyclone R-2600-13
Rating: 1,700 horsepower

FIREPOWER:
As many as 14 .50-caliber machine guns and a 75mm cannon, up to 5,400 pounds of bombs, and 1 2,150-pound torpedo

DIMENSIONS:
Wingspan: 67 feet, 7 inches
Length: 53 feet, 5¾ inches
Height: 16 feet, 4¾ inches

OTHER INFORMATION:
Manufacturer: North American
Crew: 4–6
Maximum Takeoff Weight: 33,500 pounds
Ceiling: 24,200 feet
Maximum Range: 1,225 miles, fully loaded
Maximum Speed: 303 miles per hour

The North American B-25 Mitchell medium bomber operated successfully in a variety of roles in World War II. The Mitchell was used for high- and low-level bombing, in ground strafing attacks, as a torpedo plane, and for photo-reconnaissance missions.

The B-25 became famous for its part in the Doolittle Raid on Tokyo, Japan, in 1942. In the early months of the war, the Japanese advance in the Pacific seemed unstoppable. The Dutch East Indies, Singapore, Burma, the Philippines, and Corregidor fell to the Emperor's troops.

Confidence was low in America. The United States needed a boost to build up morale among its troops and civilians. A decision was made to bomb the Japanese mainland.

Sixteen B-25 Mitchells were chosen for the daring mission. Early on the morning of April 18, 1942, Lieutenant Colonel James C. Doolittle and 15 other pilots took off from the carrier *Hornet* in the Pacific. In a violent storm, from a flight deck that tossed and turned in heavy seas, the fully loaded B-25s roared into the sky. At no time did the Mitchells fly above 1,500 feet.

Six hundred and fifty miles later, the low-flying bombers reached their targets in Tokyo, Nagoya, Yokohama, and Kobe. The Japanese were caught by surprise, and though only a small amount of damage was done, the enemy was shocked. It was the first time their country had been touched during the war. (Because of the raid, Japan reassigned four fighter groups from combat in the Pacific to protect targets at home.) Americans were thrilled and confidence rose again.

Doolittle's Raiders ran out of fuel on the return trip, as they tried to reach friendly airfields in China. They had to ditch their planes and all the B-25s were lost. Although

20

several crew members were captured by the enemy, most (including Doolittle) eventually made it back to the United States.

The B-25G model was the first airplane to be fitted with a 75-millimeter cannon. It was the largest gun ever mounted on an airplane during the war. The cannon was 9 feet, 6 inches long and weighed 900 pounds. Each shell was 23 inches long and weighed 15 pounds. Along with up to eight machine guns in the nose alone, this version of the Mitchell had enough firepower to sink small ships. It was also used in strafing runs against enemy airfields. As attack bombers, the B-25s flew low over the water and released their bombs, which exploded against the hulls of enemy vessels.

The B-25H, with 14 .50-caliber machine guns as well as a 75-millimeter cannon, was the most heavily armed airplane ever built. It was mainly used against enemy shipping and for ground strafing. The B-25J was used in high-altitude precision bombing. More of these models were produced than any other version.

BOEING B-29 SUPERFORTRESS

American—World War II

SPECIFICATIONS

ENGINE:
Number: 4
Manufacturer: Wright
Model: Cyclone R-3350-23 18 cylinder
Rating: 2,200 horsepower each

FIREPOWER:
Up to 13 .50-caliber machine guns, 20,000 pounds of
bombs and/or one 20mm cannon

DIMENSIONS:
Wingspan: 141 feet, 3 inches
Length: 99 feet
Height: 27 feet, 9 inches

OTHER INFORMATION:
Manufacturer: Boeing
Crew: 10 to 14
Maximum Takeoff Weight: 135,000 pounds
Ceiling: Over 35,000 feet
Maximum Range: 4,100 miles, fully loaded
Maximum Speed: Over 350 miles per hour

The Boeing B-29 Superfortress was a long-range heavy bomber built during World War II. Its main purpose was to end the war in the Pacific by strategic bombing of the enemy's homeland, its industries and cities.

The B-29 was the largest and heaviest airplane of its time. With a wingspan of over 141 feet, it could carry up to 20,000 pounds of bombs. Fully loaded, the Superfortress weighed 135,000 pounds and had a range of over 4,000 miles.

It was the first bomber to have pressurized cabins for the crew at high altitudes. Three pressurized compartments, each with normal atmospheric pressure, were connected together by a crawl tunnel over the non-pressurized bomb bays.

The B-29 was also the first bomber with a remote-controlled gun aiming and firing system. It carried up to 13 .50-caliber machine guns and a 20-millimeter cannon.

In 1944 the Superfortress began bombing Japan from Pacific bases 1,500 miles away in Guam, Tinian, and Saipan. Night bombing raids were ordered in which the planes were stripped of all guns and ammunition so they could carry more bombs. The Japanese defenses were weak and American losses were small.

These raids caused major damage to the enemy. Each B-29 carried six to eight tons of M-69 fire bombs. They hit the target just before dawn from a low altitude of 5,000 to 8,000 feet. Then they flew home in daylight. In one attack over Tokyo, on the night of May 25, 1945, 198 Super-fortresses wiped out 18.9 square miles of that city.

The raids were so frequent and so successful that by July 1945 B-29s were flying unchallenged over Japan. American planes dropped leaflets announcing in ad-

vance where they would strike next so that civilian lives could be saved.

Even though their industries and major cities were almost totally destroyed by bombing raids, the Japanese were prepared to fight to the last man. To shorten the war, President Truman ordered two B-29s to use atomic weapons in combat, the only airplanes in history to do so. The Enola Gay, named for the pilot's mother, dropped a single bomb on Hiroshima on August 6, 1945. The result was 78,150 dead, 13,083 missing, and 37,425 injured. Three days later, another B-29 dropped a second bomb on the city of Nagasaki. Japan surrendered soon after.

B-29s were also used during the Korean War from 1950 to 1953. Bombing missions were flown against the North Koreans and the Chinese Communists. They were part of the United Nation's force (made up mainly of Americans) which supported South Korea.

LOCKHEED C-121 CONSTELLATION
American —1940s–1950s

SPECIFICATIONS

ENGINE:
Number: 4
Manufacturer: Wright
Model: R-3350-34 Turbo Compound
Rating: 3,250 horsepower each

ACCOMMODATIONS:
Up to 106 passengers, or freight, equipment, or cargo
totaling more than 40,000 pounds

DIMENSIONS:
Wingspan: 123 feet, 5 inches
Length: 116 feet, 2 inches
Height: 24 feet, 9 inches

OTHER INFORMATION:
Manufacturer: Lockheed
Crew: 4–11
Maximum Takeoff Weight: 133,000 pounds
Ceiling: 25,000 feet
Maximum Range: 5,500 miles
Maximum Speed: Over 350 miles per hour

The Lockheed Constellation has been called one of the great airplanes of all time. In nearly 20 years of continuous production, through the 1940s and 1950s, many versions of the "Connie" were built. Each new model grew in size, power, amount of cargo, and number of passengers it could carry.

The Constellation was first flown in 1943 as a military transport during World War II. Once the war was over, it was built as a commercial airliner carrying people from place to place. The Air Force continued to use the Constellation as a cargo and staff transport. They called it the C-121.

The Connie had a unique triple rudder tail which made it easy to recognize. Its wing design, with a span of over 123 feet, was adopted from the Lockheed P-48 Lightning fighter plane. Passageways in the wings allowed the engineer to reach all engines while the plane was in flight. The Connie's high speed and low fuel use eliminated refueling stops and increased its range.

The Air Force C-121s were produced with heavier flooring, removable seats, and attachments for hospital stretchers. When the Soviet Union blockaded the city of Berlin in 1948, the C-121s joined other military transports in airlifting food and supplies to Berliners.

Some C-121s were used for transporting officials on long missions. One Constellation, the "Columbine," was used as a flying White House during most of President Eisenhower's term in the 1950s. This specially equipped Connie had an airborne teletype machine and air-to-ground telephones. Its high-frequency radio allowed the President to contact Washington from anywhere in the world. It carried the most advanced radar and navigation instruments of the day.

A crew of 11 manned the Columbine and it was always ready to fly at a moment's notice in case of an emergency. Eight men guarded the President and were responsible for his safety. The Commander-in-Chief sat at his desk or relaxed in one of two soft leather swivel chairs onboard the aircraft. A bar and full kitchen served food and drink to the Presidential guests. Eight berths provided sleeping accommodations and two couches could be made into beds.

Other versions of the C-121 transport were used as radar planes and as air ambulances. One was equipped to catch live insects in flight from New Zealand to Antarctica as part of a science project. Many were used as weather planes and flew into the center of hurricanes to learn more about these fierce storms.

29

BOEING B-47 STRATOJET
American—Late 1940s–1960s

SPECIFICATIONS

ENGINE:
Number: 6
Manufacturer: General Electric
Model: J47-GE-25 Turbojets
Rating: 6,000 pounds of thrust each

FIREPOWER:
• 2 radar-directed .50-caliber machine guns and
  20,000 pounds of bombs
        or
• 2 20mm cannons in tail section and 20,000 pounds
  of bombs

DIMENSIONS:
Wingspan: 116 feet
Length: 109 feet
Height: 28 feet

OTHER INFORMATION:
Manufacturer: Boeing
Crew: 3
Maximum Takeoff Weight: More than 185,000 pounds
Ceiling: Over 35,000 feet
Maximum Range: More than 3,000 miles, fully loaded
Maximum Speed: More than 600 miles per hour

The Boeing B-47 Stratojet was the first jet bomber ever produced with swept-back wings. Six General Electric Turbojet engines, each with 6,000 pounds of thrust, powered this high-altitude medium bomber.

A pair of jet engines hung under each wing on both sides of the fuselage. Another engine was mounted under each wing tip. The 35-degree angle of the wings added speed to the Stratojet, which flew over 600 miles per hour.

Fully loaded, the B-47 weighed nearly 200,000 pounds. To help get it off the ground, 18 1,000-pound thrust rocket units were mounted in the fuselage behind the wing. These gave the big plane an added burst of power during takeoff. In later versions, 33 of these JATO (Jet-Assisted Takeoff) units were used and later dropped off once the bomber was in the air.

During landings, a 32-foot-diameter parachute was released after touchdown to help slow the B-47. This was called the drag chute. The 16-foot deceleration chute was used as an air brake. It brought the Stratojet down to landing speed as it flew the last part of the approach pattern.

Later versions of the B-47 were fitted with in-flight refueling equipment. The Flying Boom system, developed by Boeing, allowed fuel to be passed through a tube from a tanker plane to the Stratojet while in midair.

A crew of three manned this powerful bomber. They sat in a pressurized forward compartment in front of the wing. The pilot and copilot sat under a clear, Plexiglas canopy, similar to those in fighter planes. The copilot served as the tail gunner. The bombardier sat in the nose of the bomber and acted as the navigator.

The B-47 could carry up to 20,000 pounds of bombs, including atomic weapons. It flew so fast and so high that successful attacks from enemy fighter planes were only possible by following from behind. Because of this, two .50-caliber machine guns or two 20-millimeter cannons, depending on the model, were located in the tail section. A radar fire-control system detected targets approaching from behind and gave a warning to the crew in the forward compartment. The system then tracked the other craft, positioned the guns or cannons and fired when the target came into range.

B-47 Stratojets first flew in 1947 and were used by the military throughout the 1950s. Weather versions of the bomber were active into the late 1960s.

BOEING B-52H STRATOFORTRESS
American—1950s–1980s and beyond

SPECIFICATIONS

ENGINE:
Number: 8
Manufacturer: Pratt and Whitney
Model: TF-33-P-3 Turbofans
Rating: 17,000 pounds of thrust each

FIREPOWER:
- 1 6,000 round-per-minute 6-barrel 20mm cannon and 60,000 pounds of bombs
        or
- 20 air-launched cruise missiles (ALCMs)
        or
- 20 short-range attack missiles (SRAMs)

DIMENSIONS:
Wingspan: 185 feet
Length: 160 feet
Height: 40 feet, 8 inches

OTHER INFORMATION:
Manufacturer: Boeing
Crew: 6
Maximum Takeoff Weight: 488,000 pounds
Ceiling: 55,000 feet
Maximum Range: More than 10,000 miles
Maximum Speed: 650 miles per hour

The Boeing B-52 Stratofortress was first built in 1952 as a high-altitude long-range heavy bomber. Its swept-back wings had a 35-degree angle and it was powered by eight jet engines.

Many different models of the B-52 were produced. The final version of the series was the B-52H, which was last built in 1962. Over the years, the H model has been improved and modernized. But from the beginning it was different from the others in three main ways.

This Stratofortress was the first to use the powerful Pratt and Whitney TF33 Turbofan engines. With 17,000 pounds of thrust each, they gave the B-52H an increase in range and speed. This was proven when one Stratofort flew from Okinawa, Japan, to Madrid, Spain, in less than 22 hours. That's 12,519 miles without stops or refueling!

The second change in the H model was in the tail guns. Instead of a four-gun tail turret, the Stratofort had a powerful, 6,000-round-per-minute 6-barrel 20-millimeter cannon, also called a Gatling gun.

The third change was in the frame of the airplane. It was redesigned and strengthened to fly low-level missions as well as high-altitude ones.

The B-52 can carry many different kinds of weapons. It was used as a regular bomber in Vietnam, dropping thousands of pounds of bombs on enemy targets each day.

Some Stratoforts were armed with two jet-powered air-to-surface Hound Dog missiles. The 42-foot-long Hound Dog had a 500-mile range and flew at an altitude of 50,000 feet.

Today Stratoforts carry as many as 20 air-launched cruise missiles (ALCMs), which have a 1,500-mile range. All ALCMs are controlled by an Offensive Avionics System

(OAS) computer onboard the plane. The navigator and radar navigator use this sytem to direct missiles at various targets.

Short-range attack missiles (SRAMs) are also carried by B-52s. These 14-foot-long missiles are armed with nuclear weapons.

Crew members nicknamed the Stratofortress "Buff," which stands for "Big, Ugly, Fat Fellow." It has a wingspan of 185 feet and weighs nearly 500,000 pounds when fully loaded. The crew of six stays in the forward compartment during missions since the rest of the plane isn't pressurized.

The B-52H can carry a large payload of weapons at high speeds over long distances anywhere in the world. It has advanced electronics, radar, weapons, and navigation systems. This makes the Stratofortress a valuable aircraft that is still widely used today in the United States Air Force Strategic Air Command (SAC).

BOEING 707
American — Late 1950s–1970s

SPECIFICATIONS

ENGINE:
Number: 4
Manufacturer: Pratt and Whitney
Model: JT3C-6 Turbojets or JT3D-1 Turbofans
Rating: 12,500 or 17,000 pounds of thrust each

ACCOMMODATIONS:
From 110 to 189 passengers, depending on tourist or first-class seating, plus baggage compartments

DIMENSIONS:
Wingspan: 130 feet, 10 inches
Length: 144 feet, 6 inches
Height: 38 feet, 8 inches

OTHER INFORMATION:
Manufacturer: Boeing
Crew: 4
Maximum Takeoff Weight: 248,000 pounds
Ceiling: Over 35,000 feet
Maximum Range: Over 3,000 miles
Maximum Speed: About 600 miles per hour

The Boeing 707 was the first jet airliner built in the United States. Since its earliest flight with Pan American airlines in 1958, the 707 has helped change the air passenger business forever.

The speed, range, and comfort of passenger jets made piston-engine aircraft a thing of the past. The more powerful jet planes could take off carrying a much heavier load and fly twice the distance.

Among the first to see this advantage was the United States Air Force. They called the military version of the 707 the KC-135 tanker/transport. It was used as a tanker to refuel their Strategic Air Command (SAC) B-52s in flight. As a troop transport, it carried up to 80 men or more than 35 tons of cargo. A specially designed version called "Air Force One" was used to transport the United States President, beginning with John Kennedy in 1961.

Four jet engines were mounted separately on the 707, two under each swept-back wing. Several versions were built, differing from each other in size, power, and range. The 120 and 220 models were used mainly for trips within the United States. The larger, more powerful 320 and 420 models were designed for intercontinental flights throughout the world.

"Tower to Flight 22. You are cleared for takeoff."

The pilot of the 707 released the brakes and guided the nose of the big jetliner down the middle of the concrete runway. He quickly scanned the many dials and gauges in the cockpit. Each engine must pull its share of the load if the jet was to take off successfully.

As the plane's speed increased, the passengers were pushed back into their seats. The pilot pulled the nose up slowly and the 707 lifted into the air.

40

"Gear up," said the copilot. The landing gear wheels were raised up into their compartment under the fuselage.

"Flaps up." The flaps were lifted to once again become part of the smooth wing's surface.

The big jet climbed easily through the clouds and into bright blue skies. It reached a cruising speed of more than 550 miles per hour. The ride was smooth and quiet.

Passengers gazed out their windows, comfortable in the 72-degree-pressurized cabin. Outside, only a few inches away, the temperature was more than 60 degrees below zero.

Hours later, the plane landed easily and the passengers departed, thousands of miles from where they began their journey. It soon flew on to a new destination, ready to do it all over again the next day.

The 707 was the first of many Boeing airliners which today service customers throughout the world.

LOCKHEED C-130 HERCULES
American—1950s–1970s

SPECIFICATIONS

ENGINE:
Number: 4
Manufacturer: Allison
Model: T56A-7 Turboprop
Rating: 4,050 horsepower each

ACCOMMODATIONS:
- 92 combat-equipped troops
        or
- 64 paratroops
        or
- 70 stretcher patients and 6 attendants
        or
- 40,000 pounds of equipment and supplies

DIMENSIONS:
Wingspan: 132 feet, 7 inches
Length: 97 feet, 9 inches
Height: 38 feet, 3 inches

OTHER INFORMATION:
Manufacturer: Lockheed
Crew: 4
Maximum Takeoff Weight: More than 155,000 pounds
Ceiling: 23,000 feet
Maximum Range: 2,300 miles, fully loaded
Maximum Speed: About 370 miles per hour

The Lockheed C-130 Hercules was the first military transport with turboprop engines. The plane's four propellers
were driven by turbines which were operated by jet
engines.

In production since the middle 1950s, the Hercules
completed many different jobs for the United States
armed services and more than 37 countries in the world.
It could carry 92 combat troops or 64 paratroopers. As a
flying hospital it held 70 stretcher patients with 6 attendants. The C-130 also transported up to 40,000 pounds of
equipment, supplies, and cargo.

It was used as an in-flight refueling tanker, a search
and rescue aircraft, a weather plane, and a Red Cross
relief plane. Over a two-year period during the Vietnam
War, Hercules transport planes airlifted more than one
billion pounds of supplies into Vietnam.

One model of the C-130 was fitted with special ski
landing gear coated with Teflon plastic. It landed on
ice and snow in Antarctica, carrying explorers deep
into uncharted territory.

Another model handled search and rescue work,
which included astronaut recovery from land and water.
A special nose-mounted system allowed pickups of
people or objects weighing up to 500 pounds while
the airplane was still in flight.

The Hercules delivered single loads of up to 14,000
pounds by quick touch-and-go landings or flying four
to five feet above the ground. The cargo was quickly
lowered through the large rear ramp door with the use
of a ground hook or by parachute.

The chunky, square fuselage was over 97 feet long. The
huge cargo area was more than 41 feet long, over nine
feet high, and 10 feet wide. The C-130's high wings al-

lowed the fuselage to sit close to the ground. The flat cargo floor was the same height as the floor of a standard American truck. Its low level provided for easy loading and unloading.

The Hercules had two large side doors. The rear door opened in flight and allowed vehicles or freight to be dropped by parachute. While the plane was on the ground, one part of the rear door dropped down to form a loading ramp.

The C-130 had the ability to take off within 900 feet and land in just 600 feet. One even made 21 successful landings and takeoffs from the deck of the aircraft carrier *Forrestal*. It set a world record as the largest airplane to ever operate from a carrier.

In 1976, a C-130 Hercules carried Israeli commandos to Entebbe in Uganda for the daring and successful rescue of hostages.

LOCKHEED C-141 STARLIFTER
American — Mid-1960s–1980s

SPECIFICATIONS

ENGINE:
Number: 4
Manufacturer: Pratt and Whitney
Model: TF33-P-7 Turbofans
Rating: 21,000 pounds of thrust each

ACCOMMODATIONS:
Total payload: 70,847 pounds
• 154 troops
>   or
• 123 paratroops
>   or
• 80 stretcher patients and 16 sitting wounded
>   or
• freight

DIMENSIONS:
Wingspan: 159 feet, 11 inches
Length: 145 feet
Height: 39 feet, 3½ inches

OTHER INFORMATION:
Manufacturer: Lockheed
Crew: 4
Maximum Takeoff Weight: 316,600 pounds
Ceiling: 41,600 feet
Maximum Range: 4,600 miles, fully loaded
Maximum Speed: 571 miles per hour

The Lockheed C-141 Starlifter was the first long-range jet-powered cargo plane ever produced. It was also the first transport aircraft to include a computer as a standard part of its on-board equipment.

The Starlifter was the largest cargo plane in the air when it first flew in 1963. It had a maximum weight of over 300,000 pounds, a wingspan of nearly 160 feet and a length of 145 feet.

The first models were delivered to the Military Airlift Command (MAC) in 1965. The C-141s were immediately put into service flyng men and tons of supplies on a daily basis into Vietnam. They carried 154 troops or 123 fully equipped paratroopers. These planes were also used as flying hospitals and could hold 80 patients in stretchers and 16 wounded in seats.

As a low-level combat drop plane, the C-141 would fly in low under enemy radar and drop off men or supplies. Then it would pull up fast and fly away before enemy guns had a chance to fire. It had the ability to climb quickly to high altitudes and fly at speeds of over 500 miles per hour. One Starlifter set a world record of 70,195 pounds for heavy cargo drops.

The C-141 had a high swept-back wing on which were mounted four Pratt and Whitney turbofan engines, each with 21,000 pounds of thrust. The huge cargo area was 70 feet long, 10 feet wide, and nine feet high. Two paratroop doors were in the back end of the cabin, one on each side. A large rear ramp allowed for straight-in cargo loading at truck-bed height. The ramp was opened in flight for air drops.

Most C-141s were enlarged in the middle 1970s. The volume of their cargo compartments was increased by about one-third. In addition, all Starlifters were fitted with

air-refueling equipment, giving them unlimited range.

One C-141 was operated by the National Aeronautics and Space Administration (NASA). This plane became a flying laboratory, carrying a 15,000 pound, 36-inch telescope. In the air at high altitudes, the telescope was a thousand times more accurate than on the ground because there's no atmosphere to block the view. It provided information about the planets, the sun, comets, and far-off stars and galaxies.

In 1973, three C-141s brought the first of 143 American prisoners of war back from Vietnam. Other Starlifters transported supplies and equipment to scientists at the South Pole. The C-141 became the first jet transport to land on the ice in the Antarctic.

ROCKWELL INTERNATIONAL B-1B

American—1980s and beyond

SPECIFICATIONS

ENGINE:
Number: 4
Manufacturer: General Electric
Model: F101-GE-100 Turbofans
Rating: 30,000 pounds of thrust each, with afterburner

FIREPOWER:
Total payload: 115,000 pounds
- 24 Short-range attack missiles (SRAMs) (8 more SRAMs can be carried under the fuselage)
    or
- 75,000 pounds of bombs

DIMENSIONS:
Wingspan: 136 feet, 8½ inches extended, 78 feet, 2½ inches swept back
Length: 150 feet, 2½ inches
Height: 33 feet, 7¼ inches

OTHER INFORMATION:
Manufacturer: Rockwell International
Crew: 4
Maximum Takeoff Weight: 389,800 pounds
Ceiling: 50,000 feet
Maximum Range: 6,100 miles
Maximum Speed: More than 1,320 miles per hour

51

The Rockwell International B-1 supersonic long-range bomber was designed to replace the Boeing B-52. Although smaller than the B-52, the B-1 can carry double the load and travel faster than twice the speed of sound, more than 1,320 miles per hour.

The B-1A model first flew in 1974. Its high cost and uncertain effectiveness led President Carter to cancel the program in 1978. President Reagan reinstated it in 1981 and production of the B-1B model is expected to continue into the 1990s.

Powered by four General Electric turbofan engines, the B-1B has a movable swept-back wing. For takeoffs and slower flight, the wings are fully extended and measure 136 feet, 8½ inches. For high speeds they sweep back to a 65-degree angle and a span of 78 feet, 2½ inches.

The B-1B's main role is high-speed low-level bombing. It is designed to fly as close to the ground as possible so it won't be picked up on enemy radar.

The Radar Cross Section (RCS) is a way to describe how objects show up on radar screens. RCS is measured in square meters. The lower the RCS, the harder the plane is to see on radar screens. For example, the RCS for the B-52 is 40 square meters.

The B-1B was redesigned to eliminate sharp edges and corners to make the plane less visible on radar. This is called "stealth" technology. Its RCS is now .4 meter, 100 times smaller than the B-52!

The entire structure of the B-1B, as well as its internal engineering equipment, is hardened to withstand nuclear explosions. In an enemy attack, the B-1B must be able to get off the ground immediately. After an alert is sounded, the bomber's four-man crew race to their aircraft. The first onboard presses a button on the nose gear. This is the

rapid-start system. All four engines start together automatically. By the time the crew is belted in, the B-1B is ready for takeoff. A matter of seconds could save the plane from destruction by enemy missiles!

At takeoff, each engine (with its afterburner) will develop 30,000 pounds of thrust. Once airborne, computers determine engine power settings and monitor the fuel. The pilot and copilot have their own fighter-type control stick and complete set of throttles.

The B-1B has the most advanced electronics, radar, and weapons systems available today. They guide the plane to its destination and help the pilot complete his mission—the destruction of enemy targets. Three big bomb bays carry 24 short-range attack missiles. Eight more are carried under the fuselage.

Instead of replacing the B-52s of the Strategic Air Command, B-1B bombers will join with them and the B-2 Stealth bomber. These three airplanes will form the backbone of America's air defense system into the next century.

LOCKHEED C-5 GALAXY
American—1970s—1980s and beyond

SPECIFICATIONS

ENGINE:
Number: 4
Manufacturer: General Electric
Model: TF39-GE-1 Turbofans
Rating: 41,000 pounds of thrust each

ACCOMMODATIONS:
Total payload: 220,000 pounds
• 75 troops in rear upper deck and 270 troops on lower deck
     or
• tanks, helicopters, trucks, missiles
     or
• other freight

DIMENSIONS:
Wingspan: 222 feet, 8½ inches
Length: 247 feet, 10 inches
Height: 65 feet, 1½ inches

OTHER INFORMATION:
Manufacturer: Lockheed
Crew: 5
Maximum Takeoff Weight: 769,000 pounds
Ceiling: 34,000 feet
Maximum Range: 3,749 miles, fully loaded
Maximum Speed: More than 550 miles per hour

The Lockheed C-5 Galaxy is the world's largest airplane. It can carry heavier cargo for longer distances than any other airplane ever built. Its main job is to transport heavy military equipment and troops at high speeds to trouble spots anywhere in the world.

First flown in 1968, the giant Galaxy is nearly 248 feet long, with a wingspan of almost 223 feet. The C-5 stands over 65 feet high. That's equal to the height of a six-story building!

It carries a cargo of 220,000 pounds and has a maximum takeoff weight of 769,000 pounds. Fully loaded, the Galaxy can fly nearly 4,000 miles. Empty, it can fly nonstop for over 7,000 miles. If refueled in the air, the C-5 can fly as long as the crew can last.

The Galaxy's cargo floor alone is longer than the first flight made by the Wright Brothers in 1903. The main cargo compartment has a length of 121 feet. (Orville Wright flew 120 feet.) Its width is 19 feet with a height ranging from 9½ feet to 13½ feet.

A typical freight load might consist of two M-60 tanks, or one tank and two Bell Iroquois helicopters. The Galaxy could carry five personnel carriers, one 2½-ton truck and a quarter-ton truck, or 10 Pershing missiles.

When not in use as a freighter the C-5 has seats for 75 troops in the rear part of the upper deck and can carry 270 troops in the lower deck. Cargo doors and ramps at both ends of the airplane allow straight-in loading and unloading of large equipment. The nose flips up to allow access to the front cargo area.

The C-5 can land on a 4,000-foot dirt runway. It can airdrop loads of more than 200,000 pounds. The Galaxy's advanced electronics equipment can pinpoint target areas at night or in bad weather.

Affectionately called "Fat Albert" by its crews, the C-5 played an important part in the Yom Kippur War of 1973 between Israel and its Arab neighbors. Both sides suffered heavy losses in the first week of the war but the Soviet Union airlifted supplies and equipment to the Arabs. The United States wanted to even the odds.

A massive airlift flew equipment directly from the U.S. to Israel with one refueling stop in the Azores. That's a distance of 7,500 miles each way or 15,000 miles round-trip.

C-5s and C-141 transports carried over 22,000 tons of supplies in 566 trips. Galaxys flew 145 of the missions but carried nearly half of the total tonnage. By the time both sides agreed to a cease-fire, C-5s had airlifted tanks, cannons, howitzers, helicopters, and parts of airplanes.

New wings were installed on all C-5s in the 1980s to extend the life of each airplane by 30,000 flight hours. That's equal to 30 more years of peacetime flying. Because of this, the Galaxy will be in use well into the next century.

NORTHROP B-2 STEALTH
American—Late 1980s and beyond

SPECIFICATIONS

ENGINE:
Number: 4
Manufacturer: General Electric
Model: F118-GE-100
Rating: 19,000 pounds of thrust each

FIREPOWER:
Total payload: 75,000 pounds
• 16 Short-range attack missiles (SRAMs) and advanced
  cruise missiles
          or
• nuclear bombs and weapons

DIMENSIONS:
Wingspan: 172 feet
Length: 69 feet
Height: 17 feet

OTHER INFORMATION:
Manufacturer: Northrop
Crew: 2
Maximum Takeoff Weight: About 250,000 pounds
Ceiling: 50,000 feet
Maximum Range: More than 7,000 miles
Maximum Speed: About 600 miles per hour

The Northrop B-2 Stealth long-range bomber is a giant flying wing, shaped like an arrowhead. Its main job, in addition to carrying bombs, is to be nearly invisible to enemy radar. The purpose of the B-2 is to penetrate enemy defenses without being detected, destroy enemy targets, and then head back to the United States or to safe bases in friendly countries.

Stealth is a way of designing an airplane so it doesn't show up on radar. It must have smooth surfaces, and no angles or corners. There should be no exposed intakes or exhausts since all of these reflect radar waves. Engines and fuel tanks are internalized, inside the body of the plane. Weapons are also carried inside the aircraft. They include short-range attack missiles (SRAMs), advanced cruise missiles, and nuclear bombs.

Shape rather than size is important in radar detection. The Radar Cross Section (RCS) of the B-1B bomber is .4 square meters. An average-size man walking would show up as 1.0 square meters. The RCS of the B-2 bomber is .01 square meters on the radar screen. That's equal to the RCS of a large bird and $\frac{1}{100}$ that of a man!

The B-2 is coated with radar-absorbing material (RAM) which soaks up radar energy instead of reflecting it. The RAM is stronger than steel but weighs less than aluminum and is built into the skin and frame of the aircraft.

The B-2 flies at subsonic speeds (below the speed of sound) at about 600 miles per hour. Its range is more than 7,000 miles without refueling.

The giant wing stands 17 feet high and is 69 feet long. The wingspan is 172 feet. The highly-sloped two-man cockpit has wide, wraparound windscreens. Each crew member has a fighter-type control stick and set of throttles. A fly-by-wire flight control system makes adjust-

ments automatically.

The surface of the plane is a dull blue-gray color and is curved and rounded everywhere. Large, flat surfaces are avoided because they reflect on radar screens.

Some experts question whether Stealth technology will really work. Many are opposed to the huge cost of each airplane, which is now more than $530 million.

The B-2 bomber first flew on July 17, 1989, and is still in its testing phase. If Congress approves funding for the project, full production of the B-2 would begin in the 1990s. The plane is to be operational into the next century.

GLOSSARY

Afterburner—A device attached to the tailpipe of the engine which uses hot exhaust gases to burn extra fuel for more thrust.

ALCM—Air-launched cruise missiles; they have a 1,500-mile range.

Atomic bomb—An extremely destructive type of bomb which unleashes the energy of the atom.

Azores—A group of Portuguese islands west of Portugal.

Blockade—To cut off or isolate a particular area.

Bombardier (bom-bar-DEER)—The person who operates the bombsight and releases the bombs.

Bomb bay—The compartment in a bomber where the bombs are kept; when the bomb bay doors are opened, the bombs are dropped.

Bombsight—An instrument for aiming bombs dropped from an aircraft.

Caliber—The diameter of a bullet; the inside diameter of the gun barrel.

Ceiling—The maximum altitude at which the airplane should normally fly.

Commercial—Profit-making.

Converge—To move toward each other or toward the same point.

Escort—Fighter planes which accompany bombers or other planes and fight off enemy attacks.

Exhaust—Passage through which the used gases from the cylinder of an engine escape or are expelled.

Flak—Bursts of fire from anti-aircraft guns on the ground.

Flaps—Movable sections hinged to an airplane's wing usually used to lessen speed.

Frequency—Used in radio and television transmission; measurement for electromagnetic waves.

Fuselage (FEW-suh-lahj)—The main body of an airplane.

Horsepower—A unit for measuring the power of an engine.

Hound Dog missiles—Jet-powered air-to-surface missiles; they are 42 feet long, with a 500-mile range.

Howitzer—A short cannon which fires shells in a curved path.

Intake—Passage through which air is taken in to mix with fuel in the cylinder of an engine.

MAC—Military Airlift Command.

Massive—Large and heavy.

Monitor—To watch or check on something.

NASA—National Aeronautics and Space Administration.

Navigation—The method of determining position, course, and distance traveled.

OAS—Offensive Avionics System; an electronic aviation computer which controls weapons guidance and delivery.

Payload—The bomb load of an aircraft.

Piston engine—An engine powered by pistons; pistons are solid metal pieces in the cylinder moved by a rod which is connected to the crankshaft; the movement of the pistons is sent on to the crankshaft.

Plexiglas—A clear, lightweight substance used as a cockpit cover for airplanes.

Pressurized—To keep a normal atmospheric pressure inside an airplane at high altitudes, so the crew and passengers can breathe properly.

Propeller—Rotating shaft fitted with angled blades which provides thrust in air and propels an airplane forward.

Radar—Device that determines location and distance of objects by ultra-high-frequency radio waves.

Range—A specific distance.

RAM—Radar-Absorbing Material; soaks up radar energy instead of reflecting it.

RCS—Radar Cross Section; a way to describe how objects show up on radar screens.

Reconnaissance (ree-KAH-na-sans)—The art of obtaining information about an enemy area; a survey or examination.

Rudder—Used to steer an airplane.

SAC—The Strategic Air Command of the United States Air Force.

Sloped—Slanted.

SRAM—Short-range-attack missiles; they are 14 feet long and armed with nuclear weapons.

Stealth—A way of designing an airplane so it doesn't show up on radar.

Strafing—To attack with machine-gun fire from low-flying aircraft.

Strategic bombing—Continuous attacks on enemy population centers and industry to destroy their ability to continue fighting.

Subsonic—Slower than the speed of sound (which is 660 miles per hour at high altitudes).

Supersonic—Faster than the speed of sound (which is 660 miles per hour at high altitudes).

Technology—Applied science; science put to practical use.

Teletype—Messages sent through a typewriter.

Throttle—A device which regulates the amount of fuel in the engines.

Thrust—To push forward with force.

Turbine—An engine driven by the pressure of steam, water, or air against the curved blades of a wheel or set of wheels.

Turbofan—A fan driven by a turbine in a ducted fan jet engine.

Turbojet—A jet engine in which the energy of the jet operates a turbine which in turn operates an air compressor.

Turboprop—A jet engine which operates a turbine which in turn drives the propellers.

Turret—Clear, Plexiglas half-globe in which guns are mounted.